The Gray Flannel Tramp Grows Nostalgic

Written By
MAURICE K. ISAAC

Illustrated By
MATTHEW E. ISAAC

Copyright © 2016 by Maurice K. Isaac.
All Rights Reserved.

Published by Eye of Infinity.
Printed by Lulu Press, Inc.

ISBN: 978-0-692-77368-0

First Printing.

The Gray Flannel Tramp Grows Nostalgic

Written By
Maurice K. Isaac

Illustrated By
Matthew E. Isaac

EYE OF INFINITY

GRAY FLANNEL TRAMP

Dedicated to

My Father
for
teaching me so much by example.

Contents

Foreword 7

A Hint of Stocking Top 11
English Garden 15
Father's Words 17
Killer Bees 21
Duvets 23
Passwords 25
Bear With Me 27
English Fields 29
Cornish Beaches in Summer 31
Big Bend Border 33
Postmaster 35
Movies With My Wife 37
Memorial Car 41
In a Fog 43
Daisy Chains 47
Bell's Palsy 49
Spitting Images 53
Wildlife Bridges 57
The Caver 59
Opera Translated 63
Lost 65
Cranes 67
Pubs 69

Secrets 71
Home's Memories 73
Carolers 75
Silence 77
Turner's "St. Michael's Mount" 79
Nature's Solace 81
Winter Impressions of Pembrokeshire 83

Addendum 87

Illustration Glossary 91

Foreword

As a pre-baby boomer I grew up in Bristol, England, with rationing and bomb sites a constant reminder of the war. Life for my parents was a struggle, but in many ways much simpler than today. Money was short, choices were few, spare time was minimal and goals were clear. Children were not cosseted as they are now. We played in the street, participated in contact sports without a thought, climbed trees and made bows and arrows from bamboo canes. We spent as much time out of doors as possible, exploring parks, fields, streams and rivers. We picked wild strawberries and blackberries, collected nuts and conkers and were generally much closer to nature than today's children.

As we got older, we became even more adventurous, ranging far from home on our bicycles and caving in the Mendip Hills south of town.

There were no TVs, no computers, no mobile phones and no "Social Media." Our communication with others was face to face, not anonymously through electronic devices, so we had to learn how to get along and accept the consequences of our interactions.

In this my third book, "The Gray Flannel Tramp Grows Nostalgic," advancing age, dislike of many so called technical advances, and the first indications of a failing body, have caused me to indulge my feeling that, despite all our material comforts, "we are not as happy as we used to be."

Some of the poems were inspired by memories of people and events in my childhood in England and early years in the US, others by recent observations while hiking in the backwaters of the UK. Many express my conviction that, as we have become more and more separated from nature, we no longer experience the relaxation, comfort, and renewal it can bring.

There is a recurring theme throughout the book that the explosion of new digital devices, far from making our life richer and more enjoyable, has filled it with useless, time consuming, activities and endless, pointless, impersonal communication, thereby robbing us of many simple joys, challenges, and pleasures, and facilitating the dangerous intrusion of government into our daily lives.

However, readers should perhaps remember these words of caution from Marcel Proust "Remembrance of things past is not necessarily the remembrance of things as they were."

Maurice K Isaac
Houston
July 2016

The
Gray Flannel Tramp
Grows Nostalgic

A Hint of Stocking Top

Nostalgic voyeurs all would say,
It was a disappointing day,
When stockings merged with panties, to
Become a single garment few
Red blooded men found to their taste.
Weaved with no space from toe to waist,
It covered up the female form,
And rapidly became the norm.
Ubiquitous, safe, "pantyhose."

No more that wait for legs to cross,
To "accidentally" glimpse the tops
Of stockings, and a little thigh.
No bated breath, while skirts rode high
Enough to see the darker band,
That indicated joy at hand.
No exciting clipped suspender,
Made the male libido wander.
A tragic end to sexy clothes.

And as for pointed high heeled shoes,
Accentuating female thews,
Covered by nylons to the thighs,
Whose dark seams men and women prized,
To point of drawing them with ink,
To make the unobservant think,
That silken whispers were at hand,
What male libido could withstand,
Such demonstrations of foreplay.

Don't think that they were unaware,
Or even that they didn't care.
It was a calculated tease,
An unsuspecting man to please.
A female mating ritual,
That every young buck thought was cool,
Like bra accentuated breasts,
Or buttocks by tight skirts compressed,
To make imagination stray.

By this I don't intend to say,
That men were innocent. No way!
For most would be a "peeping Tom,"
Had they the courage and aplomb
To drop pretense of innocence,
Admit their natural prurience,
And revel in the joy of sights
In which the simplest man delights.
Godiva's shame be here to stay.

Though fashions, mores, both may change,
And what was normal, now seem strange,
The sexual drive will find a way,
Put female wares upon display.
An ankle flash, a velvet mole,
Decolletage that could console
A regiment of mummy's boys,
With corsets, bustles, other ploys,
To overcome naivete.

English Garden

Our council house, when new, had not
A garden, but a building lot.
The top soil buried underneath,
No vegetation, not a leaf.
My father picked and shoveled dirt,
Until his every muscle hurt.
He trenched the yard from north to south.
Good soil he finally dug out.
Then leveled and amended it
With mulch, and even horse's shit,
Until he had a place to start
The plantings that would be a part
Of magic memories I hold,
Golden summers, winters cold.

A lawn outside our window spread,
Backed by two trees with apples red.
Herbaceous borders round it grew
With plants perennial and new
Each season. Asters, lavender,
Hydrangea, baby's breath there were.
In springtime snowdrops, daffodil
And hyacinth the beds would fill.
Then lupines, phlox, carnations pink,
Snapdragons, poppies, red and slender,
Chrysanthemums for autumn splendor.

The flowers were nice but we must eat.
Beyond the lawn, in columns neat,
Grew carrots, peas and runner beans,
Climbing around the stakes that leaned
Together, tied by father's hand
Each spring, with optimism grand,
That we would have a bumper crop,
And every vine would reach the top.
In serried ranks were brussels sprouts,
Which, after frost, without a doubt,
Tasted more sweet than any since.
Then onions, cabbages, Prince
Edward spuds, beets, lettuce, radish.
Childhood tastes that still can ravish
Memory's worn and jaded palate,
Till any appetite is hard to whet,
With produce that is no more fresh,
Than chutney sent from Bangladesh.

Father's Words

My father was a clever man
Who often, with an air dead pan,
Delivered lines of comic verse,
Or single liners somewhat terse.

To teach, by rote, life's lessons clear,
For every child with wit to hear,
Remember and internalize.
His rhyming code memorialize.

"Move me I'm burning," words so wise,
Indictment, much to my surprise
Of selfishness, and pride, and sloth.
Let's "cut our clothes from better cloth."

"As I was going up the stair
I met a man who wasn't there,"
Which warns us all we should ignore
A man without a moral core.

"The boy stood on the burning deck,
His feet were covered in blisters"
A prayer for constancy, by heck,
From child, to youth, to mister.

"As I was going to St Ives
I met a man with seven wives"
Advice monogamy is best,
And use your wits in any test!

"I see said the blind man," is a cry
For every mother's son to try
Precision in his choice of words,
When talking to pedantic nerds.

"I see it all, some of it" and
"It's clear as mud" demand
That exposition be precise.
Confusion always has a price.

"The shades of night were falling fast"
Reminds us, when the day is past,
We should repair us to our beds,
To knit once more the raveled threads.

And so, with humorous litany,
He taught us how we might be free
From all life's pitfalls and excess,
Avoid its sorrows and its mess.

Killer Bees

What became of killer bees,
Spreading north just as they pleased?
Did they succumb to northern queens,
Their offspring tamed by northern genes?
Fall in love with northern flowers,
While away the sunny hours,
Lost in exotic honey dream,
Where only frozen flowers gleam.
Die in arboreal forests far
From equator, southern star,
Overdose on foreign pollen,
Lose their stings in Texas oilmen.
Give up their military esprit,
Let dreams of great Bee Empire be.

Duvets

In hotels, B and Bs, throughout the land,
 Ubiquitous, the duvet reigns supreme.
Yet I, and fellow travelers, cannot stand
 Its thickness, and beneath it steam.
We toss it off, and then begin to freeze,
 Too hot, too cold, with nothing in between.
As loin cloth, feet and chest still feel a breeze,
It gives no heavenly comfort, no sweet dream.
 Upon its imposition I'll wage war.
 Strip it, and use the covers as my sheet.
Toss the offending innards on the floor,
And trample them beneath imperious feet,
 Until at last, dishonored, it is sent
 Back to the European continent.

Passwords

The **password**, once a two edged sword,
A secret, memorable word,
Used to distinguish friend from foe,
A magic key to let one go
Into a golden treasure hoard,
Where ageless guardian dragon snored,
Or forty thieves stored lucre free.
But Ali's "Open Sesame,"
Has now become our nemesis.
To save our assets from abyss,
We must compile, remember well,
A pseudo word unbreakable.
From four to six, eight symbols long,
Numbers with letters make it strong.
Upper, lower case, please jumble,
Punctuation, thieves won't rumble.
How to remember such a key,
Is a great mystery to me,
And so I write it on a sheet
Of paper, copperplate, so neat.
Store in drawer next to PC
Where thieves can find it readily.

Bear With Me

Bears have a widespread iconography
Expressed on flags and coins artistically.
Amazing ursine strength and habits garner
Respect from shaman, warrior, mother.
Star gazers honor them as constellations

Bears also feature large in literature,
Especially stories for the immature,
And children who loved Mowgli's friend Baloo,
Rupert, Paddington and Winnie-the-Pooh,
Still read these classics to their small relations.

Teddy from his wilder dreams could never
Excise the incident which would, forever,
Determine future generation's favorite toy.
Delighted in their "Teddies," they enjoy
Yogi Bear and Boo-Boo's conversation.

Polar bears, the largest of the family,
Over ice and snow move threateningly,
Living on seals along the sea ice interface,
And should their numbers fall or keep apace,
Realpolitik measures population.

Black bears are smaller, mostly vegetarian,
Living in forests eating fruits and carrion,
And honey, insects, berries, nuts and salmon,
Colored in shades from black to cinnamon,
Keeping heart rate down for hibernation.

Brown bears inhabit America, Eurasia,
Ranging Alaska, Russia, and Mongolia.
Omnivorous as any man, they eat
Whatever they can find, but seldom meat.
Named "Bruin" if you've no imagination.

Pandas are native to the Chinese forest.
Alas so very few of them are left.
Now zoos must advertise as panderers,
Dangling new mates for bamboo munchers,
Assigning cubs to foreign institutions.

Koalas are not truly bears but grouches,
Odd, gray, marsupial, their cubs in pouches.
Arboreal, they dwell in eucalyptus trees,
Low-energy, nocturnal, stuffing leaves.
Australians' cuddly Teddy substitution.

English Fields

Intricately patterned, colors changing,
Kaleidoscopic, green to gold to brown.
Size, shape, in random interweaving,
Give mother earth an eiderdown.
Sown by the work of many farmer's hands,
Dark hedgerows, trees, and dry stone walls combine,
To quilt, and outline, all the long tamed land,
Wildness constrained by "Harvest Man's" design.
Yet cultivation sullies nature's plan.
Though fields have structured beauty of their own,
Souls miss the ancient forests, moors, that ran
From coast to coast, while yet the "Hunters" roamed.
When God's pure rain and un-tilled soil grew
Wild flora, virgin, plentiful and new.

Cornish Beaches in Summer

Beds of gold humus, fallow for a night,
That freshly sprout, on sunny August day,
A multicolored host of flowers bright,
Planted by those, whose lack of clothing may
Mark them as worshipers of Phoebus ray.
Strange farmers, who will never pray for rain,
And, if it comes, will pack their plants away,
Leaving the beach at mercy of the main.
No lover of my fellow man en masse,
Close set the bodies, tents and screens oppress.
Gray, silent, through their happy noise I pass,
And pray, that far from this chaotic mess,
I find a small beach inaccessible,
Where we'll drink wine, alone, compatible.

Big Bend Border

It may be "Rio Grande" in spate,
Alas, on every other date,
Its flow, at best, I'd call sedate,
A barrier quite inadequate.

Yet at Big Bend its power it showed.
How, given time, it could erode,
Two canyons worthy of the name,
Bouquillas and great Saint Helene.

Across this trickling boundary
Flow economic refugees,
Illegal, uninvited guests,
That some of us regard as pests.

And, though their backs are seldom wet,
By guards and fences they are met,
For sovereignty we must protect,
Teach them to show our laws respect.

Yet there are those most welcome here,
In fact, they can be free from fear,
And, naked, wander to and fro
In desert heat and winter snow.

Silently, stealthily at night,
To make their homes on Chisos heights,
They cross the river unobserved,
And find a habitat preserved.

For bears and lions find the park
A haven, where they make their mark,
Oblivious to the ways of man,
Who only fellow humans bans.

Postmaster

Our mailboxes, adjacent to the street,
New brick or metal, ancient painted wood,
Drunkenly leaning, or upright, neat,
Are mostly stamped, as proof that they are good,
"***Approved by the Postmaster General***."
Even mine own, the oldest on our drive,
Beneath white crusted paint, still bears this seal.
In such small ways officialdom survives.
This office, "**Postmaster**," this sinecure,
Next highest paid after the "President,"
Predates the declaration that insured
Our freedom from bad British Government.
Ben Franklin the first, most famous, holder,
His "Franking" privilege made him bolder.
Most sexist office, bar the President,
Yet "**Postmistress**" might cause an argument.

Movies With My Wife

Our Friday evening ritual, dinner
And a movie show, selected turn about.
Nola, "Love Stories," and I, the sinner,
"Sex or Violence," she suffered with a pout.

So many movies I cannot recall,
Yet, three exceptions memory retains.
In San Francisco I was held in thrall,
My faith in Mozart's genius reclaimed.

Ingmar Bergman's, Swedish, "die Zauberflote."
I love the hand picked ethnic audience,
Whose eager faces, young and old, emote
To Mozart with a passion so intense.

The comic Dragon and the handsome Prince,
The Night Queen's ladies, lustfully entranced,
Sarastro's bass, never a better since,
And Papageno by his bells enhanced.

Then "Chariots of Fire," at Walnut Creek,
My expectations, oh so very low,
Her choice, "of Christianity it speaks,"
With such an intro how was I to know!!

It captured the ambitions of my youth.
The dreaming spires of Oxbridge that I sought,
Athletic prowess, learning to be couth,
And singing G and S I had forgot.

A masterpiece I never will forget,
Last, greatest, paean to the amateur,
The champagne balanced hurdles made me sweat,
Noblesse oblige romantic passions stirred.

In Houston, last, but not to her the least,
"French Kiss," that Nola never could forget.
French major, au pair, junior Francophile,
She loved diminutives that end in ette.

Meg Ryan, Kevin Kline, acting so French,
Serge Gainsbourg might his heritage renounce,
Had he not Bardot, Birkin on his bench.
Double romance, when English is pronounced,
By English speakers, as they think the French,
Seducing foreign maidens, might entice
Their victims to surrender, and so wrench
Virginity from Anglo Saxon mice.

Memorial Car

Tomorrow I get back my car.
As good as new mechanics say.
Parts sent from Germany afar,
Have reassembled been this day.

Would that my dear departed wife,
Might thus so resurrected be,
Parts from Nebraska, full of life,
New lungs a miracle to see.

So she might drive the car she chose,
Enjoy her sons, how they have grown,
And once more wear her favorite clothes,
Smell of that perfume all her own.

This miracle I'll never see,
So let this car, so dear to her,
An everyday memorial be,
The moving headstone I prefer.

In a Fog

CANTO I

Dark night of fog all traffic stilled
The city, Venice like, unwheeled
With visibility so poor
Only afoot can one be sure
To sidestep any accident,
Arrive at home sans incident.
Street lamps, footsteps, voices muffled,
Eerie figures hunched and duffled
Spell out the names of streets with care
Greet perfect strangers, if they dare,
Comment on such "fearful" weather,
Then with cold and damp they shiver,
Glad for some human company,
Show tiny speck of sympathy,
Make common cause against the fear
That, all unspoken, lurks so near
The surface of our timid hearts,
When from the norm our way departs.
Then on separate ways they fumble,
Till upon their homes they stumble.
In thankful haste rush to the door.
Once safe inside make all secure.
Then with stiff drink the body warm,
Shut out the horror till next morn.

CANTO II

From LA I have driven north
Over the mountains sallied forth.
Now down the "Grapevine," at top speed,
I rush to Bakersfield in need
Of bed, and copious sustenance,
For oil business called me hence.
Alas, where welcome lights should spread,
Lies only darkness, power's dead,
Or worse, it is that dreadful curse,
Puts many a driver in a hearse,
The Central Valley Tule fog,
More terrifying than road hogs.
I hear the squeal of brakes ahead,
Metal on metal grinds, then red
Flames through the haze appear.
It is too late for me I fear.
Yet luck is with me, anchors hold,
Despite a skid that leaves me cold,
With inches to the wreck I stop.
Unscathed then, from the car I hop
To safety, only just in time,
As following cars plow into mine.
Another Tule pile-up,
My safety record all washed up.

CANTO III

Climbing through mist, the dripping trees,
Dark and mysterious, create unease.
Do trolls or goblins lurk behind
Each gnarled trunk, and will they find
A tasty morsel for their pot?
Such silly thoughts are Tommy-rot!
And yet depressed I struggle on,
Careless joy of hiking gone.
But then I see faint light ahead,
Remember why I left my bed
So early on this foggy morn.
My boots sprout wings, and I am born
Into bright sunlight where, at last,
I see a coastal panorama vast,
Its valleys filled with cotton wool,
Once fearsome fog now beautiful.
The path along the ridge is bright
With flowers bathed in morning light.
My spirits soar, I skim the ground
And praise the lord with cheerful sound.

Daisy Chains

Do somewhere children still make daisy chains,
Or play at conkers, and dam up the creek,
Pick flowers, jump in puddles when it rains,
Play marbles, kick the can, or hide and seek?
Or is their playtime merely virtual,
In darkened rooms with screen fed images,
Never to see the world au naturel,
Twittering prisoners of their Face-book pages?
A picture of a daisy never can
Compare to feeling petals on your cheek.
No images of Hoover or Aswan
Give half the joy of plugging the last leak
In tiny dam of sticks, and stones, and clay,
Then in a moment see it swept away.

Bell's Palsy

Bi-polar, twisted, two faced grin,
Makes manifest an evil twin,
Left smile by Dali, right by Munch,
One eye open, other crunched.

Split masked Janus, sadness, joy,
Wrinkled ancient, smooth faced boy.
Cruel wages of a hidden sin,
Reveal the sadness that's within.

Its hard to see and hard to blink,
Lips non-responsive, drooling drink.
All chewing must be on one side,
No room for manners or for pride.

Good vowels, but misplaced Ps and Vs,
Loose lips sink consonants like these.
Expressions still are possible,
But grimaces are horrible.

Though it's impossible to spit,
Yet raise an eyebrow, you're a hit.
Flare one nostril, wink one eye,
Matrons, girls, no more are shy.

Affliction indiscriminate,
Heeds not the sufferer's birth date,
Or sex, or race, or other state,
Uncaring random act of fate.

What of its name, who's Charlie Bell,
To claim this bloody, living Hell?
He was an eighteenth century Scot,
Well that I'm sure explains a lot,

Two hundred years ago you say,
With no good treatment till this day.
Must wait until it goes away,
But what if it is here to stay?

Just tough it out, give us a shout
If it should last more than about
A month or two, or three or four,
Don't start to worry 'till a score.

Is it a sin transmissible,
Kisses, hugs, or careless dribble,
To family, friends, or paramour?
I feel I have to know the score.

So, all are safe, and need not quake,
Change not my habits for their sake.
Good news, and yet I fear the worst,
Will my generations be accursed.

What chance I suffer this again,
Uncomfortable, though no pain,
I'm fearful it be permanent?
Ten years and only five percent!

So, Jekyll, Hyde, stuck in mid-change,
Until my features rearrange,
I hide myself from all but friends,
Until this strange affliction ends.

If, two faced, I might end my days,
This sage advice to all I raise,
Take not for granted symmetry,
Unmatched, imbalanced, you may be.

So make a record of your face,
While everything is still in place.
Then, if you suffer Bell's Palsy,
No need rely on memory.

Spitting Images

Do widespread anti smoking laws
Extend their ban to chewing chaws,
Expectorating in spittoons,
A favorite pastime in saloons?

Chewing tobacco is more fun
Than masticating bubble gum.
But gum provides a lot of spit,
Saliva needed to permit
Our demonstrations of disgust,
Or lubricant, that soldiers must
With polish use to shine their shoes,
Make spit balls to relieve the blues.

But though it has its uses, please!
Expectoration spreads disease.
It is as dangerous as a sneeze,
So never spit into a breeze,
And never be a lick-spittle.
With pride avoid the hospital.

Sometimes, for sport, spit is controlled.
Cherry pit spitting, I am told,
Is all the rage in Michigan.
Though personally I'm not a fan,
Preferring watermelon seeds,
For higher lip ejection speeds.
Not part of the Olympics yet,
But world records have been set.

Spit on your palm to seal a deal.
Spit on a baseball, you will feel,
After a warning, umpire's zeal,
And be ejected like a heel.

Our planet's flora, quite polite,
Are spit-less, which I think is right.
Our fauna not so well behaved,
Some nasty species seem depraved.
Keep out of range of reptile spit,
But if unluckily you're hit,
Take a picture of the spitter,
Some are harmless, some are bitter.
Not much spitting by our mammals,
Definitely worst our camels.

Spit three times to ward off evil,
Jewish custom biblical.
"In spitting distance" – very near,
But not with cherry pits I fear.

"Spitting image," doppelganger,
As like as if their spit they shared.
Prescient its author, and yet stranger,
Saliva, DNA, compared!!

Wildlife Bridges

As super highways cleave the normal habitat
Of squirrels, cougars, moose, elk, deer and honey bees,
Witness a boom in unique wildlife bridges that
Connect small populations so that they may breed
In unrestricted gene pools, add diversity.
If LA's kind, green, fauna experts have their say,
Then will a landscaped overpass transect the city,
Santa Monica mountain lions cross freeways,
To impregnate lonely virgin lionesses.
In Banff the wolves, bear, deer and elk
Have more than three score crossings to transgress,
Bridges and subways, many more than human ilk.
Even in England, fallow deer can cross
Notorious orbital M twenty five,
In safety for themselves, and without loss
To humans speeding, texting, as they drive.
Toad underpasses, elevated squirrel spans,
Oslo's high hives to aid migrating honey bees,
Deutschland's green crossings of their autobahns,
Sydney's possum bridge, what clever wheeze.
Yet sadly, walking Houston, I still feel a need,
Oh let us build some armadillo bridges, please.

The Caver

CANTO I
A caver was, and is, I fear,
Poor cousin to the mountaineer,
Perhaps it's just the different gear,
Or temperament.

For cavers plumb the depths with lights,
While mountaineers essay the heights.
Horizons far, or stalagmites.
Ascent, descent.

The cavers dirty boiler suits,
Helmets, carbide lamps, hobnailed boots,
An outfit only fit for brutes,
Or troglodytes.

But climbers kit is for the strong,
Carabiners, ropes, pitons,
With slings, light boots, and helmets on.
Dressed for the fight.

Caving, nothing could be sadder,
Climbing aluminium ladders,
Filling lamps from human bladders.
So down to earth.

Climbers brave the granite's crack,
To one side feet, the other back,
Any trace of fear they lack.
Sure of their worth.

Through passage tight the caver squirms,
Yet there's a rule that all hold firm,
Do not divest till your return,
Then lubricate.

Climbers tie bowlines and belay
To trusted partners, so that they,
Falling, can live another day.
How intimate.

CANTO II

My fears are acrophobia,
And sometimes barophobia,
But never claustrophobia,
And so I cave.

French cavers always led the way,
Their father, Norbert Casteret,
With candles, diving sumps, they say.
Mon Dieu, so brave.

But not for us *grande gouffre* French,
In our backyard were caves to quench
The ardor of the greatest mensch.
The Mendip hills.

Caving on Mendip was quite rough,
Changing in dirty barns was tough,
But none of us could get enough
Of such cheap thrills.

In limestone, carboniferous,
Riddled with holes we liked to trust,
Swiss cheese not Cheddar fired our lust.
A simple vice.

Goatchurch, Swildon's, Banwell Bone,
Caverns, swallets, pots we'd roam,
Priddy, Burrington our home.
Dark paradise.

Some caves were dry and some were wet
The latter posed a double threat
Exposure, drowning, sudden death.
We weren't impressed.

Why did we do it, where the joy?
Because it was the real McCoy,
Where we might youthful skills employ,
And courage test.

With age, enthusiasm waned,
Dirt, dark, and dampness body drained,
Fatter, less supple, ached and pained,
Our joints all groaned.

We fled for surcease, to the surface,
Left dark, damp and rocky crawl space,
Smelled flowers, earth and grass embraced.
Here we were grown.

Yet now I dream of compensations sweet,
It would be quite impossible to tweet,
When buried down so many feet.
A phone free zone.

Opera Translated

"The Flute" in English, what a travesty,
Even a Philistine can surely see,
Mozart composed it for the German tongue,
And if in other language it is sung,
It loses magic, sparkle, mystery.
Though the translations may be very
Clever, accurate, and up to date,
Inevitably they adulterate
The master's genius, and so result
In such a disharmonious tumult,
That only arias of Queen of Night,
Convey true passion, angst, and dynamite.
For all those consonants have disappeared,
And only notes and vowels can be heard.

Lost

With satellites and other gear
This modern age has banished fear.
There's no excuse for being lost,
For at a very modest cost,
Your GPS can find the way,
And you need never go astray.

Yet some at such devices sneer,
Who've felt that shivery touch of fear
On lonely walks across the moor,
When sun dips down, and mists obscure
A path that once had seemed so clear,
But now begins to disappear.

It's when you know you must depend
On compass, map, and wit to bend
And to advantage use that fear,
To find your way on paths unclear,
A touch of danger thrills your sense
Makes every feeling more intense.

Though I've been lost three times before,
In snow, on mountain and on moor,
Yet I would lose myself again,
In any sort of wild terrain,
If once more I might just contrive
To feel so totally alive.

Cranes

Dark silhouettes against the rising sun,
Angular, stately, on they come,
A dozen, in formation, flying low,
Led by an airplane, ultralight and slow.
A ragged skein of whooping cranes appear,
Migrating south to warmer climes, they steer
Past silent namesakes, in the port below,
Earthbound, sullen, in regimental row,
Unmoving, till their masters turn the key,
Then cranking jerkily and noisily,
Unload the cargo from a waiting hold.
Insentient machines, by man controlled.
To call these monsters cranes insults the bird,
Whose whooping makes their disapproval heard.

Pubs

Sad schizophrenic and pretentious pubs
I drank in, as I walked the Coastal Path,
Painful anachronisms, dreadful grub,
That raised my cultural hackles and my wrath.

Dark beams and ancient pictures of St. Ives,
But ears assailed by repetitious rock,
Minimalism for uncultured lives.
Why not some shanties, Mendelssohn, Baroque?

Bars stocked with standard alcoholic fare,
Good local beers, but oft indifferent wines,
Well brands, gins, vodkas, whiskeys, only fair,
Of unsophisticated taste sure signs.

The menus as alike as peas in pod,
Sausages, pie, a curry, fish and chips,
Plaice breaded, battered, mushy peas, or cod.
Sunday, roast meat, potatoes and parsnips.

And yet, when seated at the bar, a chance
To meet some country gentry, characters,
Talk politics, and hear the local slant,
With never any violence or tears.

Secrets

If you would keep a secret
You must never write it down.
Never e-mail it or tweet it,
Never hint it with a frown.
For the government is watching
Watching you.

If you would keep a secret,
It must stay with you alone.
Never whisper, never breathe it,
Never speak it on the phone.
For the government is listening,
Is listening to you.

If you would keep a secret,
Do not think you're safe outside,
To semaphore or smoke it,
As then woe to you betide,
For the government is droning,
Is droning over you.

If you would keep a secret,
Let it in your thoughts remain.
So far they cannot take it,
Cannot pry it from your brain.
But they're working. Oh they're working.
Let us pray they work in vain.

Home's Memories

Crumbles the house in which my children grew,
In which my wife coughed out her final days.
Precious the joys and sorrows here we knew.

Here where our loved sons' childhood quickly flew,
Filled with delight, and sometimes dark dismay,
Crumbles the house in which my children grew.

Moments of loss and black despair were few,
Successes often set our hearts ablaze.
Precious the joys and sorrows here we knew.

So should I now prepare to bid adieu,
From bricks, and wood, and memories, part my ways,
Let crumble house in which my children grew.

Sell, so a philistine rebuild, renew,
Wipe clean the slate, unthinkingly erase
The precious joys and sorrows here we knew.

No, I am fired with resolution new,
To stem time's depredation and decay,
Let crumble not the house in which we grew,
Remember joys and sorrows here we knew.

Carolers

I miss the little carolers,
Forlornly standing in the porch,
Singing badly of the shepherds,
Complete with gloves, scarves, hats and torch

We paid them more to go away,
Than for the beauty of their song,
And, cutting short their tuneless stay,
We prayed "let better come along."

That was Christmas sixty years ago.
Today the music has to stop.
Children alone in dark or snow,
Our duty is to call a cop.

Now, if they come to your front door,
Lest accident steal your estate,
I'm sad to say I must implore,
Insure against unkindly fate.

Though what our Lord would have to say,
Or, what is more, what he might do,
To those who turn his choir away?
I'm glad the choice is up to you!!

Silence

Silence, a precious, rare, commodity,
Chance for its enjoyment shrinking,
Can still be found, far from the city,
In valleys where a cell phone cannot ring.
Sometimes, at night, I try to bring it near.
Close the windows, turn off lights and power,
But when the house is silent, then I hear
The traffic on the freeway, ever louder.
Timorous new world afraid of silence.
Music and chat drown out disturbing thought,
Devil's tool to keep us from the presence,
Aural distraction till we're caught.
Then, deafened by its loud cacophony,
Abandon hope of inner harmony.

Turner's "St. Michael's Mount"

Cold, damp and dreary, nasty Cornish Spring,
Unhappy children, who preferred the beach,
A darling wife, who must see "everything,"
My first impressions of "The Mount" impeached.

Crossing by boat, high tide, the causeway flooded,
Dragging struggling offspring up the cobbled road,
Playing tourist, every aspect studied,
Church, castle, history, till I must implode.

Long waiting, for the tide to rise again,
So to the mainland we could safely cross,
And dream of Normandy, across the main,
Where we might see a more impressive schloss.

For twenty years, if I would close my eyes,
St Michael's conjured up this vision,
Until, in Ireland, much to my surprise,
Friendly castle prompted great revision.

Modestly displayed upon the wall,
Turner's impression of St. Michael's Mount.
I recognized it instantly, and all
My memories were suddenly wiped out.

Dreamlike, surreal, through pale misty haze,
Impossibly steep, the mountain soars.
Above, the alabaster church conveys
A contrast to the simple sailor's chores,

Depicted in the cruel, dark, foreground,
The struggle for survival that's the lot
Of fishermen the world around.
Pray Turner's vision never be forgot.

Nature's Solace

Lying in clovered, flower be-dappled fields,
Interpreting the cries of butterflies,
The spectrum of prismatic light, that gilds
The wings of bluebottles and dragonflies
Skimming the surface of a stagnant pool,
Where frogs and sticklebacks make pregnant home,
Their coupling, procreation, Nature's rule
That every species feed the great genome.

Following primrose studded paths to sin,
Traversing gorse and purple heathered moor,
Lost in the splendor of blue-belled forests grim,
Standing in awe as pounded cliffs endure
The daily tidal onslaught that will bring
Unstoppable, inevitable, end.
Pebble on shingle grinding everything
To sand, painting the beach with magic blend.

Watching the sunset from Hawaiian heights,
Perhaps tonight the rare green-apple flash.
Braving the Arctic for cold Northern Lights,
Crossing the desert, giving camels lash.
Mirages, oasis, fresh water king,
And rain so scarce by children never seen.
From travels and experience may I wring
A feeling for things wrought by hand unseen

So to forget the sense abusing sound,
And sight, of sterile electronic life,
Traffic and talk, ubiquitous and loud.
The air we breathe with dark vibrations rife.
No silence, no music of the spheres,
Our ears belabored by uncensored noise
That must unnerve us, multiply our fears,
Unless we turn to Nature's equipoise.

Winter Impressions of Pembrokeshire

Low silver sun that pierces not the haze.
All shadows long, no matter what the hour.
I dread the shrinking of declining days.

Leafless the branches, wet the clifftop ways.
Bright golden gorse the last unshrivelled flower.
Low silver sun that pierces not the haze.

With downcast eyes I trudge, lost in a maze
Of memories and thoughts that make me cower.
I dread the shrinking of declining days.

Dawn scurries on to dusk, no noonday blaze,
The wind blows cold, I flinch before its power.
Low silver sun, still cannot pierce the haze.

My goal is far and convolute the ways.
Tired eyes and limbs, my empty stomach sour,
I dread the shrinking of declining days.

But then a single shaft of gold empowers
My spirit, softens my dour glower.
And golden sun at last dispels the haze.
I fear no more the shrinking of my days.

Addendum

Postmaster

Since I wrote this poem Megan Brennan has been appointed as Postmaster General. Her salary is $276,840 per annum which means the office is still the second highest paid after the President. As far as I know, nobody dares to refer to her as the Postmistress General.

Movies with My Wife

Serge Gainsbourg was one of the most important figures in French popular music, and an archetypal Frenchman, famous, among other things, for his two recordings of the very sexy song "Je t'aime" with Brigit Bardot and Jane Birkin.

Daisy Chains

Since hardly any of today's children make daisy chains or play conkers, a few words of explanation are necessary. Both activities though very simple in concept and execution provide endless fun.

To make a daisy chain, pick wild daisies making sure to leave length on the stem. Using a fingernail or end of a pair of scissors, carfully pierce the end of the stem and thread the end of another flower into the hole. Repeat this until you have the desired length.

Conkers is a traditional children's game played in Britain using the seeds of horse chestnut trees - the name 'conker' is also applied to the seed and to the tree itself. The game is played by two players, each with a conker threaded onto a piece of string: they take turns striking each other's conker until one breaks.

The Caver

In the fifties the most common source of light for cavers, was the carbide lamp. The design was simple but elegant. Water dripped from a small upper chamber at a rate controlled by a threaded valve onto calcium carbide in a lower chamber. The resulting interaction produced acetylene gas which expanding through a nozzle in the centre of a reflector was lit by a spark from a flint, producing a bright light. As long as the caver had water, carbide and a pricker to clean out the nozzle, some amount of light could be produced. However sometimes, in dry caves, the source of water was unconventional!

Turner's "St. Michael's Mount"

The original painting is in the Victoria and Albert Museum so the version I saw in Ireland must have been a reproduction, but a very convincing one.

Winter Impressions of Pembrokeshire

This final poem is in the form of a villanelle. Probably the most famous villanelle in the english language is "Do not go gentle into that good night" by Dylan Thomas. It is a taste of what is to come in my fourth book.

Illustration Glossary

"Those Legs" 10
Black and White Acrylic Paint
On 16 x 18" canvas

"Killer Bee" 20
Pencil and Pigmented Ink
On 11 x 14" acid-free paper

"The Family Bears" 26
Pencil and Pigmented Ink
On 11 x 14" acid-free paper

"A New Beginning" 32
Pencil and Pigmented Ink
On 11 x 14" acid-free paper

"Memorial Moment" 40
Charcoal
On 11 x 17" acid-free paper

"Two-Faces" 48
Scratch knife
On 8 x 10" scratchbord

"Cave Searching" 58
Pencil and Pigmented Ink
On 11 x 17" acid-free paper

"The Facilitated Migration" 66
Black and White Acrylic Paint
On 14 x 18" canvas

"What's Left" 72
Pencil and Pigmented Ink
On 11 x 14" acid-free paper

"The Comparison of Turner" 78
Pencil and Pigmented Ink
On 11 x 14" acid-free paper

www.ingramcontent.com/pod-product-compliance
Lightning Source LLC
Chambersburg PA
CBHW031413040426
42444CB00005B/549